Tap the Puck

Teaching Tips

Pink Level 1

This book focuses on the phonemes **/ck/e/u/**.

Before Reading

- Discuss the title. Ask readers what they think the book will be about.
- Sound out the words on page 3 together.

Read the Book

- Ask readers to use a finger to follow along with each word as it is read.
- Encourage readers to break down unfamiliar words into units of sound. Then, ask them to string the sounds together to create the words.
- Urge readers to point out when the focused phonics phonemes appear in the text.

After Reading

- Encourage children to reread the book independently or with a friend.
- Guide readers through the phonics exercises at the end of the book.

This edition is published by arrangement with Booklife Publishing.

North American adaptations © 2024 Jump!
5357 Penn Avenue South
Minneapolis, MN 55419
www.jumplibrary.com

Decodables by Jump! are published by Jump! Library.

Library of Congress Cataloging-in-Publication Data is available at www.loc.gov or upon request from the publisher.

ISBN: 979-8-88524-706-1 (hardcover)
ISBN: 979-8-88524-707-8 (paperback)
ISBN: 979-8-88524-708-5 (ebook)

Photo Credits
Images are courtesy of Shutterstock.com. With thanks to Getty Images, Thinkstock Photo and iStockphoto.
Cover – Shutterstock. 4 – Vaclav Volrab. 5 – Shooter Bob Square Lenses. 6 – Ronnie Chua. 7 – Domenic Gareri. 8 – Ronnie Chua. 9 – dotshock. 10 – Iurii Osadchi. 11 – Shooter Bob Square Lenses. 15 – Shutterstock.

Can you find these words in the book?

net

puck

tap

It is a puck.

It is a net.

Tap the puck.

Tap it to the net.

Tap tap tap!

Go go go!

Tap the puck.

It is in the net!

Can you say these sounds and draw them with your finger?

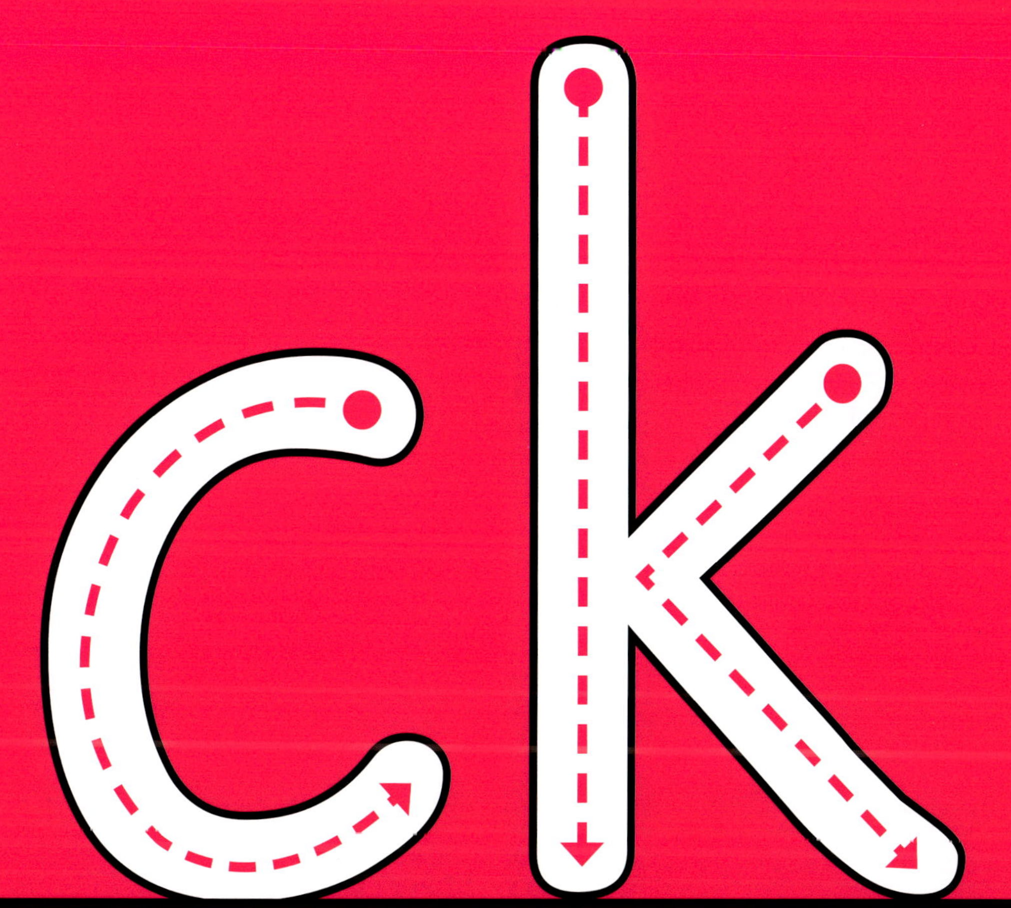
ck

Using the Letter Bank, trace the missing letter into each word.

puc__

ta__

n__t

Letter Bank

p k e

What other words do you know with the letters /ck/, /e/, or /u/?

luck

peck

truck

Practice reading the book again:

It is a puck.

It is a net.

Tap the puck.

Tap it to the net.

Tap tap tap!

Go go go!

Tap the puck.

It is in the net!